Lots of Love Lunch Box

by Joy L. Stevans

The Standard Publishing Company, Cincinnati, Ohio
A division of Standex International Corporation

Cover design by Matt Key of Keyart.
Interior design by Andrew Quach.

Printed in the United States of America

ISBN 0-7847-0521-6
UPC 7-07529-03386-0

STANDARD
PUBLISHING
Cincinnati, Ohio

Table of Contents

Introduction

The idea of napkin notes is a simple one, but one I believe can encourage your child in unimaginable ways. I began writing these notes because I would crawl into bed each night lecturing myself on all I had not said to my wonderful oldest daughter. I would wonder, "Did I even say anything *nice* to her?" Though she was helpful, funny, caring, and loving, I seldom told her that I noticed those things about her, or more than that, that I appreciated those things! I began searching for a special way to tell her how wonderful I think she is. Then I remembered . . .

There was a particular friend of mine in school who, each day at lunch, would take her napkin out of her sack lunch, read it, smile to herself, and put the napkin back in her bag. I have no idea what was on that napkin, but I have always remembered that smile. So, I began writing notes on my daughter's lunch napkin, and soon if I missed a day she was asking why I had not written her a note! As it has become a part of our daily routine, we enjoy the time the two of us share—and we are not even together! Love notes to my daughter in her lunch, on her napkin. Such a simple idea!

The following is a collection of some of the notes I have sent to my daughters over the years. These brightly colored messages are certain to lift the spirits of your child. If you do not have the time to go beyond just sending one of these notes (personalized by you and signed with an "I love you!"), you will still see your child respond to these notes. However, you may want to do a little more, and so I have included supplementary ideas for extra special lunches, as well as additional suggestions for notes that you could write on napkins.

Please keep in mind that these lunch box notes are not a replacement for your *spoken* words of encouragement, or your *physical* touches of love for your child, but they are a way to assure your child of your love every school day. Ephesians 4:29 says, "Do not let any unwholesome talk come out of your mouths, but only what is useful for building others up" *(NIV)*. With these notes of encouragement, you will find your child responding in ways you may not have imagined, and you will be reminded each day how wonderful your child is!

You are so special to so many people!

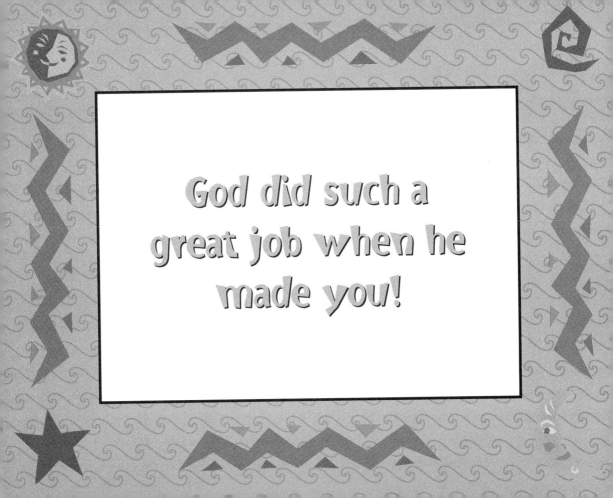

God did such a
great job when he
made you!

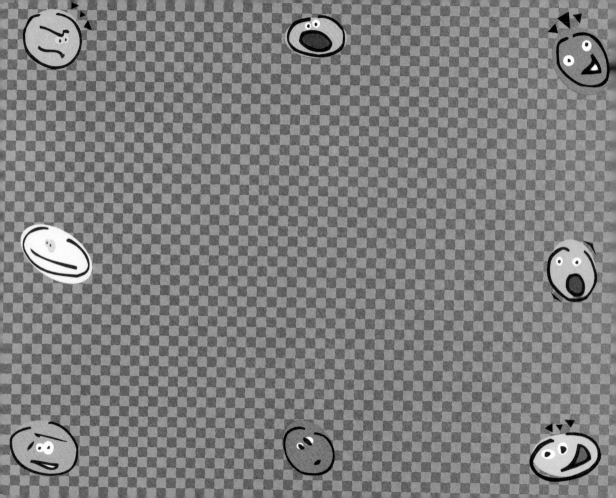

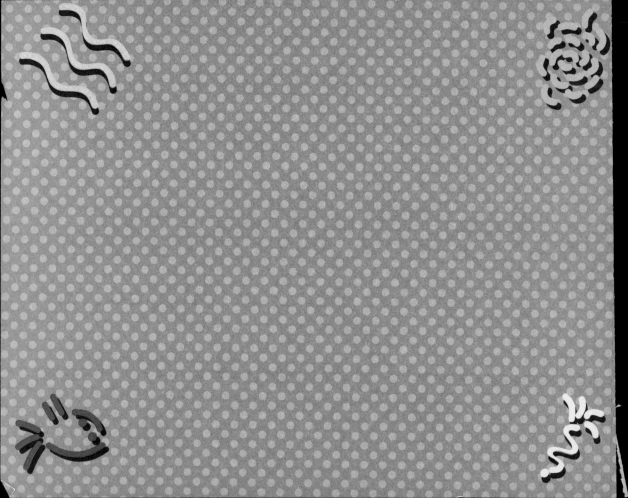

You do a great job
on your schoolwork!

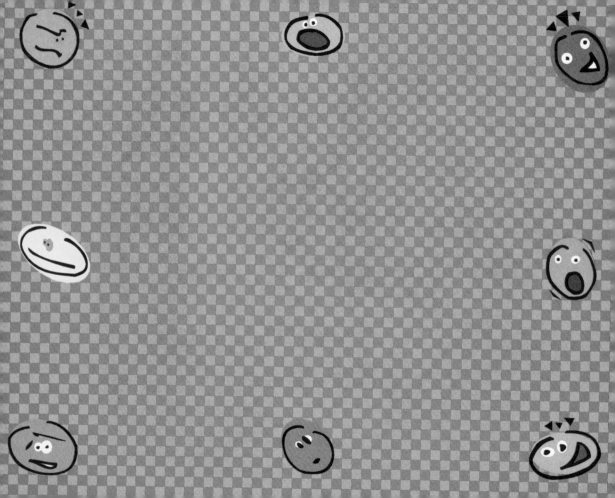

Jesus will help you do
whatever is too hard
for you today!

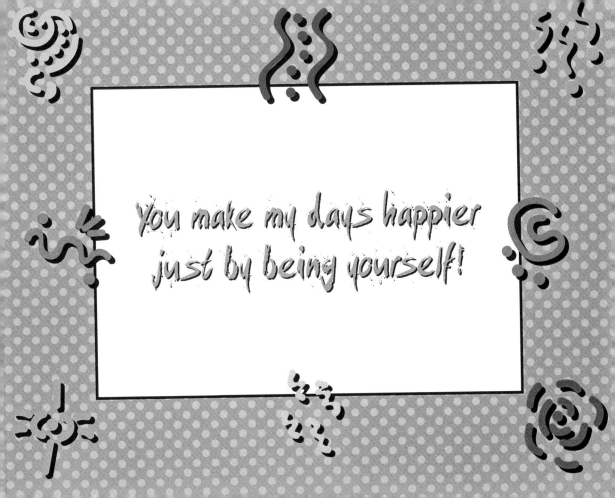

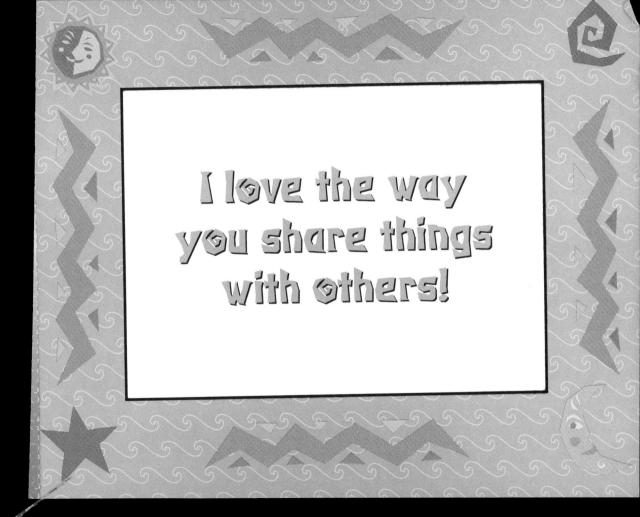

You find so many things interesting, you make me interested, too!

You choose the best colors
to color your pictures
with—and your pictures
are beautiful.

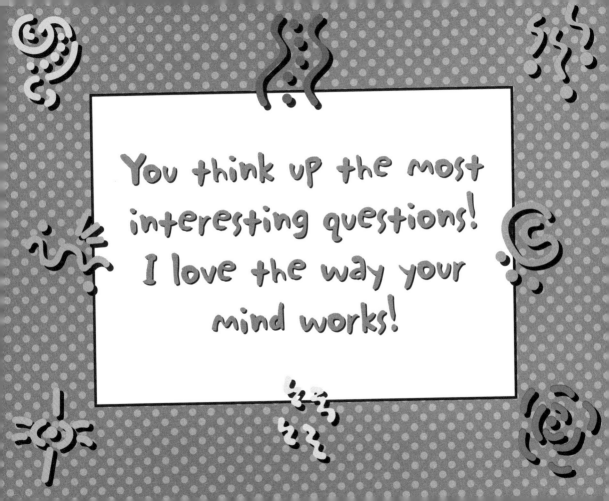

You think up the most interesting questions! I love the way your mind works!

Thanks for keeping your room clean; I really appreciate it!

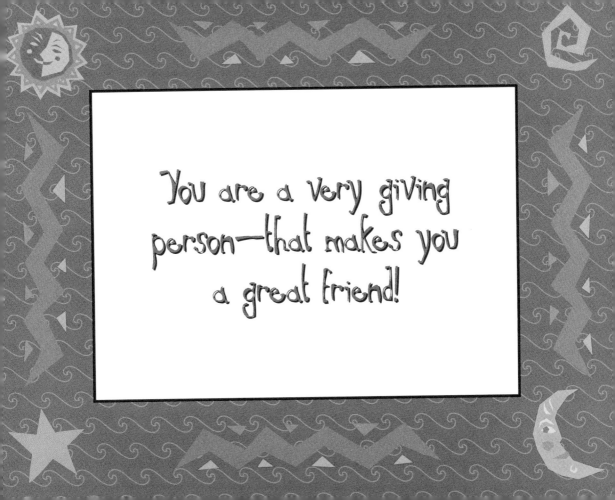

You are a very giving person—that makes you a great friend!

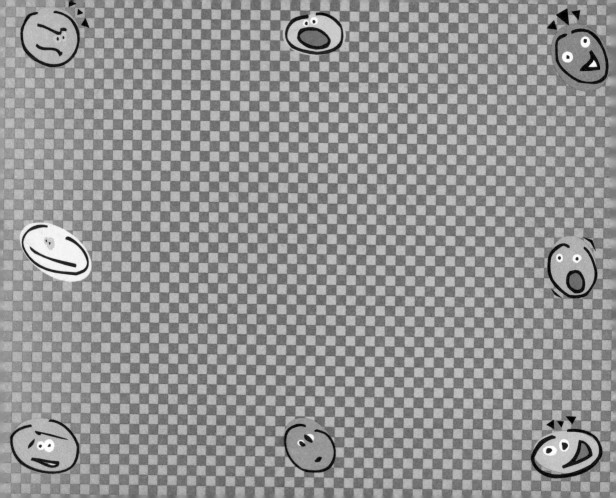

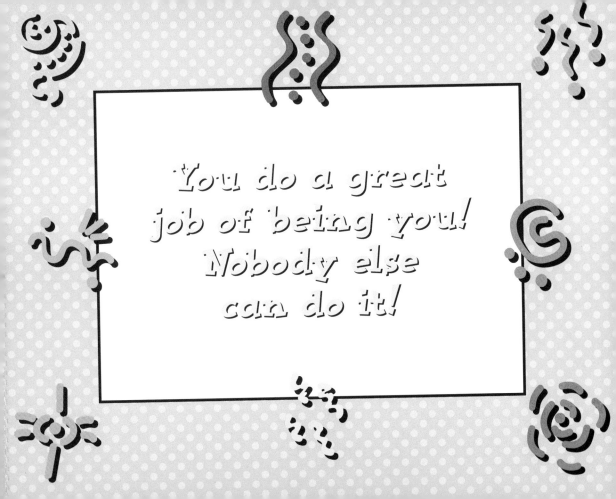

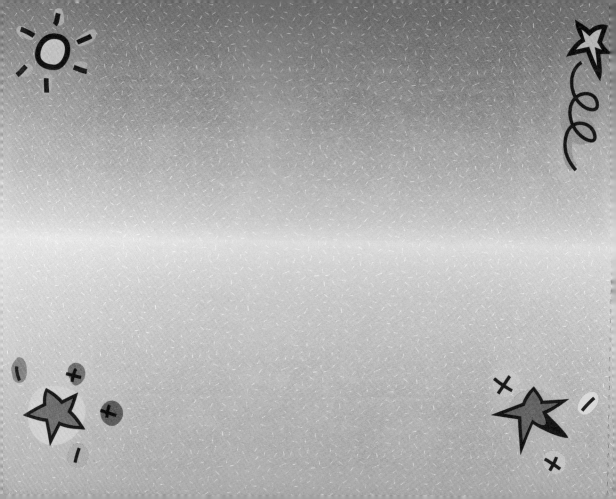

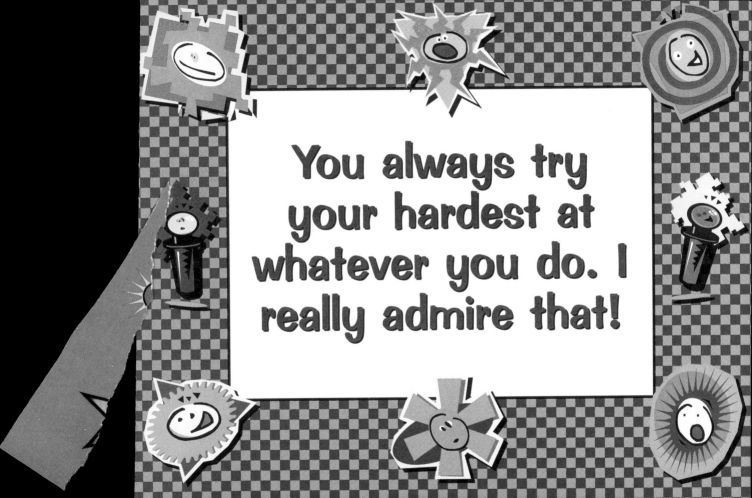

You always try your hardest at whatever you do. I really admire that!

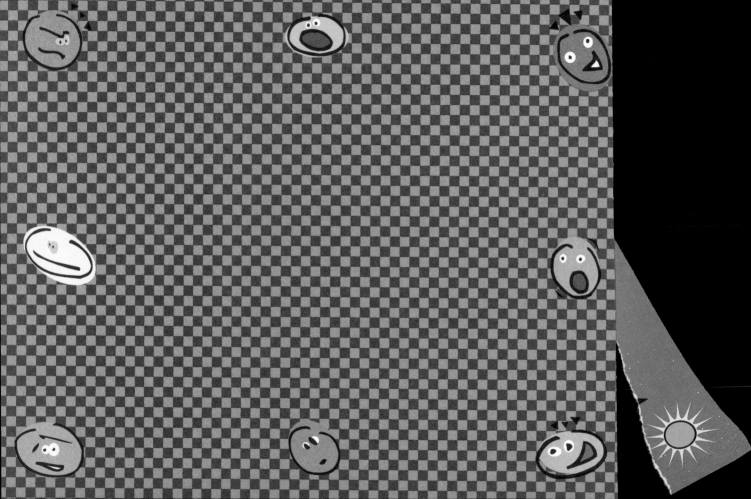

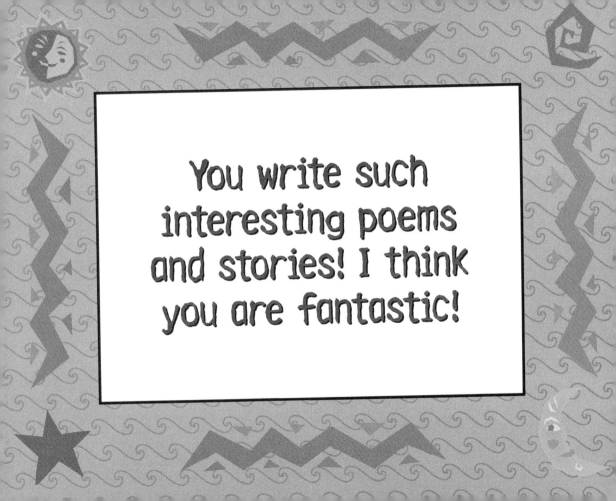

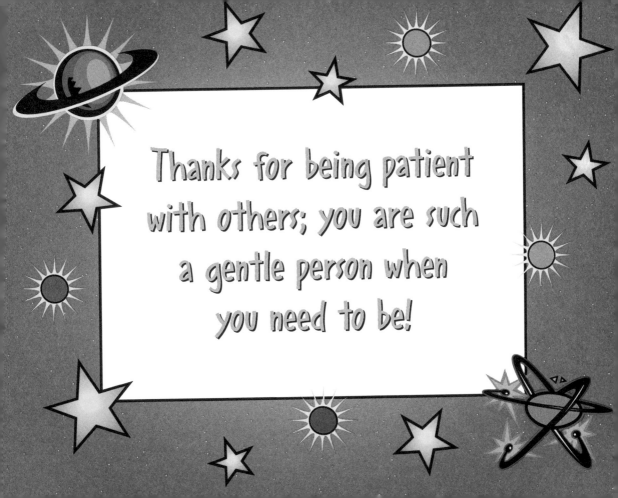

Thanks for being patient
with others; you are such
a gentle person when
you need to be!

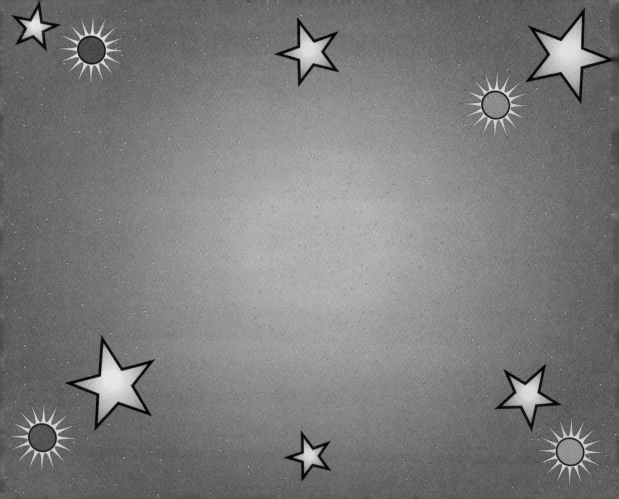

You teach me new things all the time. Thanks for being my teacher as well as my child!

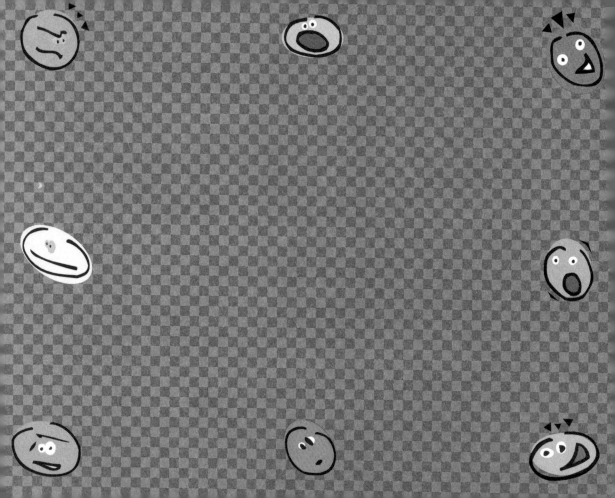

Thanks for taking such good care of your things. That makes me really proud of you!

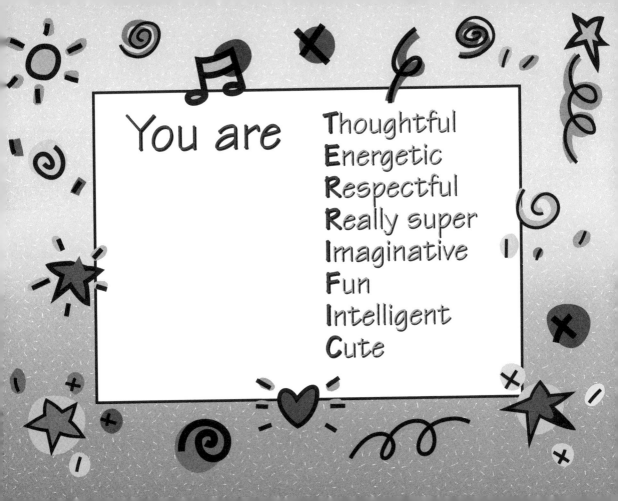

You run so fast, you are a blur! Just like on the cartoons! I wish I could run so well! I'm very proud of you!

Thanks for going to bed on time without complaining; I really appreciate that!

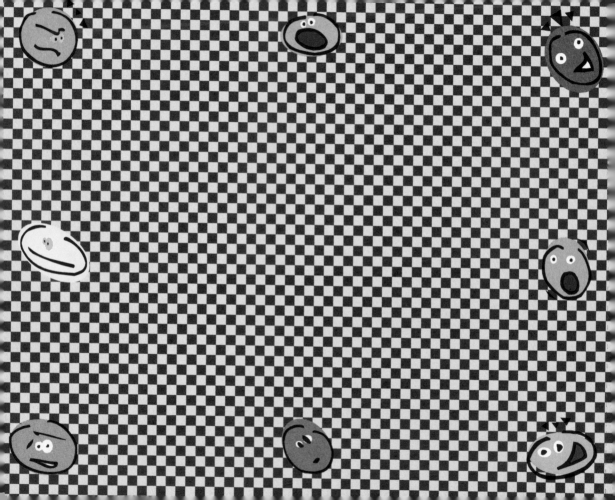

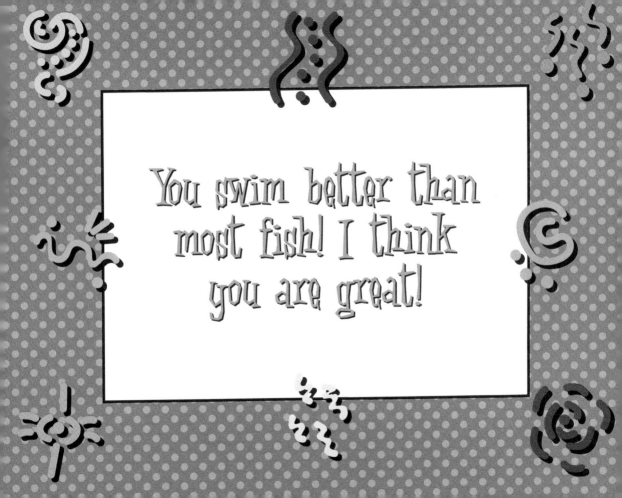

I love the way you take care of the world God gave us to live in. You make me proud!

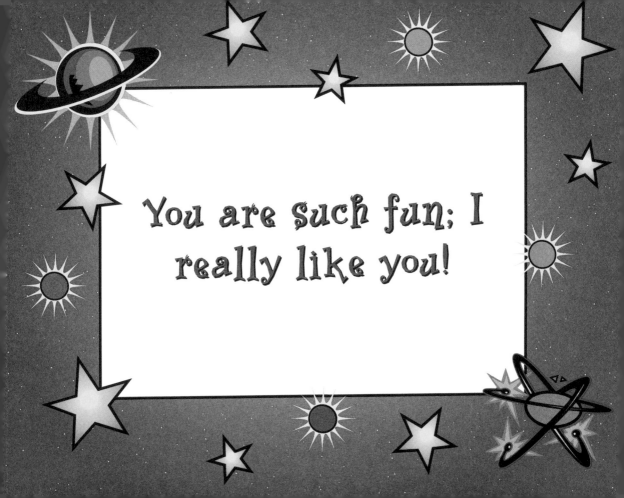

You wake up in such a good mood! It's a pleasure to be with you in the mornings!

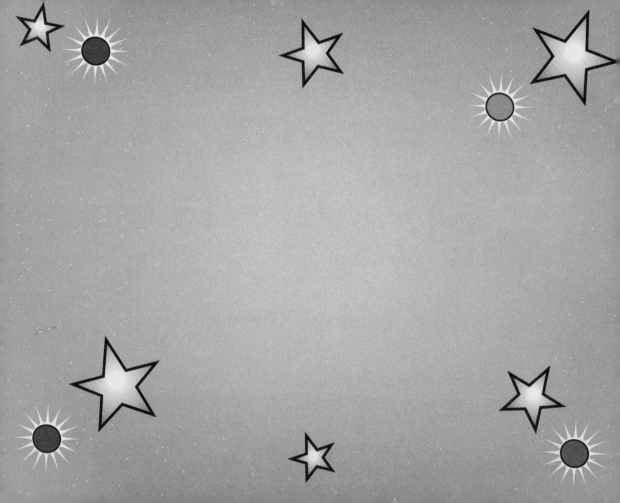

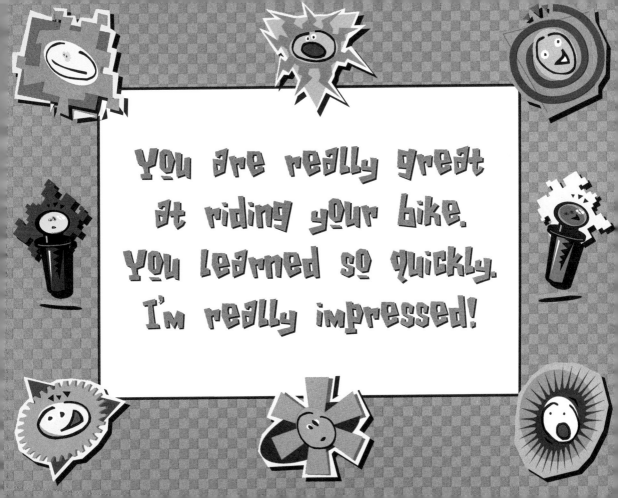

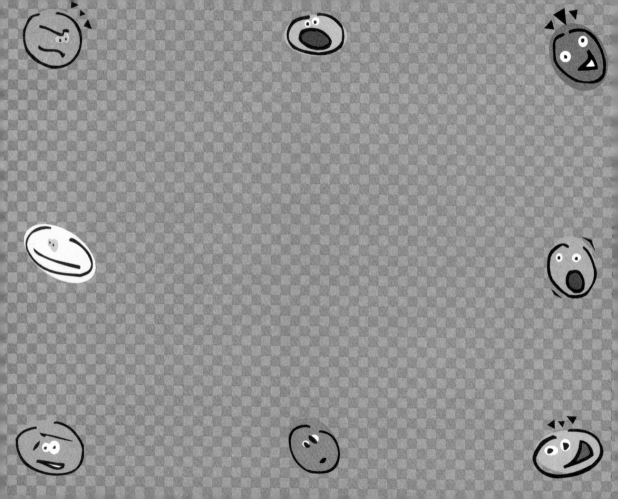

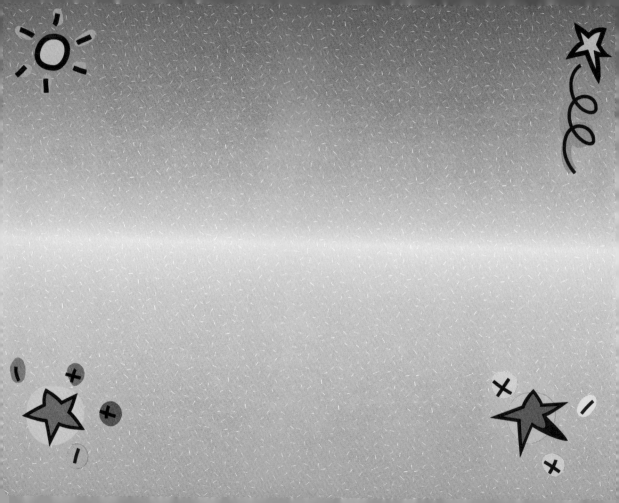

Twenty-Five Bonus Note Suggestions

These ideas are perfect for personalizing messages for your child! Make it relevant and applicable to their situations to show them how much you care.

1. Today is your first day of third grade—you are doing a great job of growing up!
2. (Draw a star and put your child's name in the center)

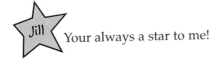 Your always a star to me!

3. No one can sing like you do; I love to listen to you.
4. You are a wonderful big sister (or brother)!
5. Idea: Make an acrostic of your child's name. For example:
   Joyful
   Outstanding
   Delightful
   Interesting
   You are all these things!
(For more ideas for acrostics see the list of alphabetized adjectives at the end of the book.)
6. Your trumpet (or violin or piano) playing is getting better and better! I'm so proud of you!
7. You are the greatest seven year old I know! I'm glad you belong to me.
8. You are a child of the King—that makes you a prince (or a princess).
9. Nobody can rattle off those football stats like you can! I think you are amazing!
10. You do a wonderful job of taking care of (insert the name of your family's pet), thank you!

11. You are a fantastic hockey player (or basketball, soccer, etc.)! I love watching you play!
12. Your younger sisters (or brothers) really look up to you. They think you are great and so do I!
13. Your freckles are one of my favorite parts of your face!
14. I'm so glad God made you the way you are! I needed a daughter (or son) just like you!
15. (Draw a boat)

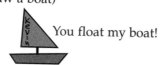 You float my boat!

16. I like the way you keep practicing your piano lessons—you are really getting better!
17. You are great at remembering songs to sing in the car; thanks for making our trips go faster!
18. You are a terrific dancer! I think it's great that you like to dance!
19. You are great at jumping rope! Have fun doing it today!
20. You make the ABSOLUTE BEST snowmen!
21. The way you decorate cookies is fantastic! You are so creative!
22. (Draw a picture of a house with smoke coming out the chimney)

 You make our house a home!

23. Whether you are using your inside voice or your outside voice, I love listening to you!
24. Your teacher told me how well you cooperate in class. That's fantastic!
25. I'm looking forward to summer when we can spend some more time together; you are great company!

Extra-Special Lunches

These are just the very beginnings of ideas—use your imagination to include the things that would mean the most to your child! Go crazy if your child would like it; keep it subtle if he might be embarrassed. The most important thing is to remember you are doing it for your child. Let your child know how wonderful he is, how fantastic you think he is, and what a good job he is doing, but above all, let him know! You won't be able to measure the value of the investment!

Here are some extra ideas which make the lunch box a little more than just a place to hold peanut butter and jelly!

- Place stickers on napkins to liven things up a bit. And don't be upset if your child puts them on the lunch box; it is the child's lunch box, not yours!
- Use different colored napkins: red and green for Christmas, bright yellow for April, and so on.
- Fill napkins with confetti for a surprise.
- Cut the napkins into shapes. Hearts, flowers, circles, diamonds—all are easy shapes that will delight your child.
- Plan a theme week each month.
  September: Add school supplies to the lunch box with appropriate love notes, such as "You make our home extra colorful" with a gift of crayons.
  October: Include a different colored leaf each day—"God made you even more incredible than this beautiful leaf!"
  November: Spend a week reminding your child why you are thankful for him.
  December: Concentrate on Christ as our best Christmas gift and include small gifts as reminders of what the season is really about.
  January: Have a week of resolutions from you to your child, such as "In 1999 I will think more carefully before saying 'no' to your ideas."

February: Spend the week letting your child be your valentine. Insert a valentine a day or extra special candy for dessert.

March: Concentrate on spring and new birth. Include a fresh flower every day or maybe little umbrellas for the drink.

April: Easter time! Cutting the napkins into a shape of a cross is a good reminder of Christ's love for your child. Notes teaching your child what the different symbols of Easter mean are a good reminder for us all; try lilies of the valley, palm branches, on an empty plastic egg to represent the empty tomb.

May: As school winds down it is a good time to spend a week giving your child special certificates for improved grades, good behavior, helpful attitude, etc.

June: Include cut out magazine pictures of things you'd like to do with your child this summer, or things he can look forward to. Remind your child how you like spending time with him.

Of course, birthday times deserve a week full of extra special napkins and lunch boxes full of confetti and ribbon! Make confetti by using a hole punch on your Sunday cartoon section. Buy curling ribbon and fill the lunch box with curly twists of ribbon so that when your child opens his lunch box, he is pleasantly surprised!

• Design a code to use for your special messages. Then your child can have fun figuring out the code as well as being encouraged. Make it a simple code, however, as most lunch times are short and the call of the playground is strong! We have used the simple 1=A, 2=B, 3=C code with success.

• Use rebus puzzles to draw out your note. One of the easiest is "I love you."

Acrostic Adjective Suggestions

Below are some suggestions for adjectives for each letter of the alphabet, with apologies to the Zoes, Xaviers, and Quintens out there! These are just suggestions; let your imagination run wild and personalize the adjectives to fit your special child!

A   athletic, adorable, able, amazing, angelic

B   beautiful, brave, bright, brainy, brilliant

C   cute, cuddly, clever, considerate, caring

D   daring, darling, diamond, delicious, dandy

E   elegant, exciting, enthusiastic, energetic, excellent

F   funny, fabulous, fun, friendly, fair

G   good, great, gentle, go-getter, giving

H   heavenly, happy, hard-working, honest, helpful

I   intelligent, inquisitive, interesting, imaginative, important

J   jolly, joke-teller, jubilant, joyful, jazzy

K   kingly, kind, keen, kid, knowledgeable

L	lovable, laughing, little, lovely, leader
M	merry, marvelous, musical, model, much-loved
N	nice, neat, nervy, nifty, nine-year-old
O	outstanding, out of this world, optimistic, original, one in a million
P	precious, perfect, pretty, prized, pearl
Q	quick, quiet, queenly, quality
R	royal, respectful, rare, responsible, radical
S	sweet, super, strong, star, special
T	ticklish, truthful, talented, thoughtful, trustworthy
U	unbelievably great, unique, understanding, unconditionally loved, utterly fantastic
V	virtuous, vivid, valuable, valiant, vital
W	wise, wonderful, winner, warm, witty
X	x-tra special, x-tremely wonderful, x-citing, x-pert, x-ceptional
Y	you're wonderful, you're loved, you're fun, you're great, yummy
Z	zestful, zippy, zealous, zooming, z-best